C000040561

Teach Your Cat
GAELIC

Funny & surprisingly clever books. Love. Love.
DAWN FRENCH, ACTOR & COMEDIAN

Anne Cakebread not only has the best name
in the universe, she has also come up with a
brilliantly funny book.
RICHARD HERRING, COMEDIAN

The cutest book I have ever seen in my life...
I'm supposed to be reviewing it and
then giving it back, but I'm afraid that's not
going to happen.
GAABRIEL BECKET, AMERICYMRU.NET

All cats know Gaelic. Everyone knows that.
They just pretend not to. "Balach math!"
SAM HEUGHAN, ACTOR, 'OUTLANDER'

Teach Your Cat

GAELIC

Anne Cakebread

Thank you to:
Helen, Marcie, Lily, Fred and Wilma,
my family, friends and neighbours in
St Dogmaels for all their support and
encouragement, Carolyn at Y Lolfa
and Beathag Mhoireasdan for Gaelic
translations and pronunciations.
Tapadh leat.

In memory of Frieda, who started us on the
Teach Your Dog journey.

First impression: 2023

© Anne Cakebread & Y Lolfa Cyf., 2023

Illustrations and design by Anne Cakebread

ISBN: 978-1-80099-339-6

Published and printed in Wales on paper from well-maintained forests by
Y Lolfa Cyf., Talybont, Ceredigion SY24 5HE
e-mail ylolfa@ylolfa.com
website www.ylolfa.com
tel 01970 832 304

I grew up only speaking English.
When I moved to west Wales, I adopted Frieda,
a rescue whippet, who would only obey
Welsh commands.
Slowly, whilst dealing with Frieda, I realised that I was
overcoming my nerves about speaking Welsh aloud,
and my Welsh was improving as a result – this gave me
the idea of creating a series of books to help others
learn languages.
You don't even have to go abroad to practise.
If you haven't got a cat, any pet or soft toy
will do: just have fun learning and speaking
a new language.

– Anne Cakebread

"Hello"

"Ha-lò"

pron:
"Ha-low"

"Come here"

"Thig an seo"

pron:
"Hig an shaw"

"Leave it!"

"Fàg e!"

pron:
"Fa-ag eh!"

"Stop!"

"Sguir!"

pron:
"Sgooth!"

"No!"

"Chan eil!"

pron:

"Chan ale!"

'Ch' as in 'Loch Ness'

"Very good"

"Glè mhath"

pron:
"Glay vah"

"Stop!"

"Sguir!"

pron:
"Sgooth!"

"How much is it?"

"Dè tha
e a' cosg?"

pron:
"Day ha
eh uh cosg?"

"Don't scratch"

"Na bi
a' sgrìobadh"

pron:

"Na bee
ah sgree-buh"

"Are you OK?"

"A bheil thu ceart gu leòr?"

pron:

"Uh vale oo key-awrsht goo lyawr?"

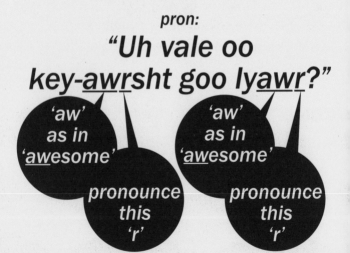

'aw' as in 'awesome'

pronounce this 'r'

'aw' as in 'awesome'

pronounce this 'r'

"Bedtime"

"Àm cadail"

pron:

"Ah-oom cad-ill"

"Goodnight"

"Oidhche mhath"

pron:
"Oo-ee-<u>ch</u>ya vah"

'ch'
as in
'Lo<u>ch</u>
Ness'

"Be quiet!"

"Bi sàmhach!"

pron:

"Bee saa-va<u>ch</u>!"

'ch' as in '*Lo<u>ch</u> Ness*'

"Wake up!"

"Dùisg!"

pron:
"Doo-shk!"

'oo'
as in
'boot',
but longer

"What's the time?"

**"Dè 'n uair
a tha e?"**

pron:

"Day noo-a̱r aha eh?"

*pronounce
this
'r'*

"Lunchtime"

"Àm lòn"

pron:
"Ah-oom lawn"

"Are you full?"

**"A bheil
thu làn?"**

pron:

"Uh vale oo lawn?"

"All gone"

"Uile deiseil"

pron:
"Oo-luh deesh-all"

"What are you doing?"

"Dè tha thu a' dèanamh?"

pron:

"Day ha oo uh djee-an_a_v"

'a'
as in
'_a_go'

"It's snowing"

"Tha e a' cur an t-sneachd"

pron:

"Ha eh coor an tnachk"

'oo' as in 'boot', but longer

pronounce this 'r'

'ch' as in 'Loch Ness'

"It's cold"

"Tha e fuar"

pron:
"Ha eh foo-ar"

pronounce
this
'r'

"It's hot"

"Tha e teth"

pron:
"Ha eh tee-eh"

"It's raining"

"Tha an t-uisge ann"

pron:

"Ha an toosh-gee-ah an"

'gee' as in 'geese'

'a' as in 'ago'

"It's windy"

"Tha e gaothach"

pron:

"Ha eh goo-ha<u>ch</u>"

'ch'
as in
'Lo<u>ch</u>
Ness'

"It's a nice day"

"Tha latha math ann"

pron:
"Ha laa mah a-oon"

"Come down!"

"Thig a-nuas!"

pron:
"Hig an-oo-ass!"

"Do you want to play?"

"A bheil thu airson cluich?"

pron:

"Uh vale oo arson cloo-ee_ch_?"

'ch' as in 'Lo_ch_ Ness'

"Do you want to play football?"

"A bheil thu airson ball-coise a chluich?"

pron:

"Uh vale oo arson ba-ool-cosha a chloo-eech?"

'a' as in 'ago'

'ch' as in 'Loch Ness'

"What have you got?"

"Dè th' agad?"

pron:
"Day ha-gut?"

"Where are you going?"

"Càite bheil
thu a' dol?"

pron:

"Kah-<u>cha</u> vale oo <u>a</u> doll?"

'ch'
as in
'<u>cheese</u>'

'a'
as in
'<u>a</u>go'

"What have
you been doing?"

"Dè bha thu
dèanamh?"

pron:

"Day va oo djee-an<u>a</u>v?"

'a'
as in
'<u>a</u>go'

"Have you got
a headache?"

**"A bheil do
cheann goirt?"**

'aw'
as in
'<u>aw</u>esome'

pron:
**"Uh vale d<u>aw</u>
<u>ch</u>ee-<u>own</u> g<u>aw</u>rsht?"**

'ch'
as in
'Lo<u>ch</u>
Ness'

'ow'
as in
'c<u>ow</u>'

'aw'
as in
'<u>aw</u>esome'

"Have you got a cold?"

"A bheil an cnatan ort?"

pron:
"Uh vale an crat-an <u>aw</u>rsht?"

'aw'
as in
'<u>aw</u>esome'

"Where are you?"

"Càite bheil thu?"

pron:

"Kah-_cha_ vale oo?"

'ch'
as in
'_cheese_'

'a'
as in
'a_go_'

"Don't be afraid"

"Na biodh feagal ort"

pronounce this 'h' slightly

pron:

"Na bee-uh fay-gal awrsht"

'aw' as in 'awesome'

"Get out!"

"Mach à seo!"

pron:
"Ma<u>ch</u> ah shaw!"

'ch'
as in
'Lo<u>ch</u>
Ness'

"Is that your favourite toy?"

"An e sin an dèideag as fheàrr leat?"

pron:
"Un ay shin an djay-djag ass yearr lyat?"

"Do you
want a cuddle?"

"A bheil thu ag
iarraidh cudail?"

pron:

'oo'
as in
'boot'

"Uh vale oo ag
ee-a-ry cud-l?"

"Cheers!"

"Slàinte!"

pron:

"Sl-ahn-tya!"

'a' as in 'ago'

"I love you"

"Tha gaol agam ort"

pron:
"Ha goo-al agam <u>aw</u>rsht"

'aw'
as in
'<u>awe</u>some'

"Happy Birthday"

"Co-là-breith sona dhut"

'Co' as in '<u>cope</u>'

pron:

"<u>Co</u>-laa-breh <u>son</u>-uh ye-oot"

'so' as in '<u>soc</u>k'

"Good luck"

"Gun tèid leat"

pron:

"Goon tyay-<u>ch</u> lyat"

'ch'
as in
'<u>ch</u>eese'

"Merry Christmas"

"Nollaig Chridheil"

pron:

"Naw-lick <u>Ch</u>ree-awl"

'Ch' as in 'Lo<u>ch</u> Ness'

"Happy New Year"

"Bliadhna mhath ùr"

pron:

"Blee-ana vah oor"

'oo' as in 'b<u>oo</u>t', but longer

pronounce this 'r'

"Thank you"

"Tapadh leat"

pron:
"Tapa lyat"

"How many?"

"Cia mheud?"

pron:

"Key-a vee-ad?"

'a'
as in
'ago'

1
one
"aon"
pron:
"uh-n"

2
two
"dhà"
pron:
"yah"

3
three
"trì"

pron:
"tree"

4
four
"ceithir"

pron:
"kay-hir"

5
five
"còig"

pron:
"co-ick"

6
six
"sia"

pron:
"she-ah"

9
nine

"naoi"

pron:
"nuh-ee"

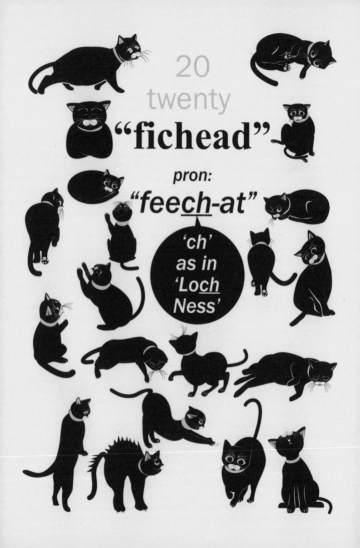

20
twenty

"fichead"

pron:

"fee**ch**-at"

'ch'
as in
'Lo**ch**
Ness'

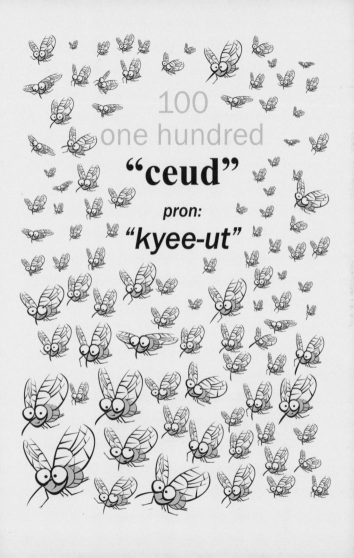

100
one hundred

"ceud"

pron:

"kyee-ut"

"Are you happy?"

"A bheil thu toilichte?"

pron:

"Uh vale oo tall-ee-chuh?"

'oo' as in 'b**oo**t'

'ch' as in '**ch**eese'

"Have you got
enough room?"

**"A bheil rùm
gu leòr agad?"**

pron:

*"Uh vale room
goo lee-<u>aw</u>r ag-at?"*

'aw'
as in
'<u>awe</u>some'

"Goodbye"

"Mar sin leat"

pron:
"Marr shin lyat"

Titles in this series include:

Teach Your Cat Cornish
Teach Your Dog Cornish
Teach Your Dog French
Teach Your Dog Gaelic
Teach Your Dog Gog: North Wales Welsh
Teach Your Cat Guernesiais
Teach Your Cat Irish
Teach Your Dog Irish
Teach Your Dog Italian
Teach Your Dog Japanese
(Rugby World Cup Travel Edition)
Teach Your Dog Korean
(e-book only)
Teach Your Cat Manx
Teach Your Dog Māori
Teach Your Dog Spanish
Teach Your Cat Welsh
Teach Your Dog Welsh

More coming soon!